The Greenwich Guide to

Measuring Time

Heinemann
LIBRARY

Graham Dolan

Royal Observatory Greenwich

H www.heinemann.co.uk
Visit our website to find out more information about Heinemann Library books.

To order:
☎ Phone 44 (0) 1865 888066
📄 Send a fax to 44 (0) 1865 314091
💻 Visit the Heinemann Bookshop at www.heinemann.co.uk to browse our catalogue and order online.

First published in Great Britain by Heinemann Library, Halley Court, Jordan Hill, Oxford OX2 8EJ, a division of Reed Educational and Professional Publishing Ltd. Heinemann is a registered trademark of Reed Educational & Professional Publishing Ltd.

OXFORD MELBOURNE AUCKLAND JOHANNESBURG BLANTYRE
GABORONE IBADAN PORTSMOUTH (NH) USA CHICAGO

Designed by Celia Floyd
Illustrations by Jeff Edwards
Originated by Dot Gradations, UK
Printed in Hong Kong/China

05 04 03 02 01
10 9 8 7 6 5 4 3 2 1
ISBN 0 431 13002 7

British Library Cataloguing in Publication Data

Dolan, Graham
  The Greenwich guide to measuring time
  1. Time measurements – Juvenile literature
  I. Title   II. Measuring time
  529.7

Acknowledgements
The Publishers would like to thank the following for permission to reproduce photographs: Pg.4 National Maritime Museum; Pg.5 National Maritime Museum; Pg.7 [both] Francisco Diego; Pg.8 National Maritime Museum; Pg.9 National Maritime Museum; Pg.10 Francisco Diego; Pg.11 Ancient Art and Architecture; Pg.12 Ancient Art and Architecture; Pg.13 Ancient Art and Architecture; Pg.14 Science Photo Library; Pg.15 Science Photo Library; Pg.16 [top & bottom] National Maritime Museum; Pg.17 National Maritime Museum; Pg.19 [top & bottom] National Maritime Museum; Pg.20 National Maritime Museum; Pg.21 [top & bottom] National Maritime Museum; Pg.22 National Maritime Museum; Pg.24 National Maritime Museum; Pg.25 [top & bottom] National Maritime Museum; Pg.26 National Maritime Museum; Pg.27 National Maritime Museum; Pg.28 National Maritime Museum; Pg.29 National Maritime Museum.

Cover photograph reproduced with permission of Telegraph Colour Library.

Spine logo reproduced with permission of the National Maritime Museum.

Every effort has been made to contact copyright holders of any material reproduced in this book. Any omissions will be rectified in subsequent printings if notice is given to the Publisher.

Contents

Any words appearing in the text in bold, **like this**, are explained in the Glossary.

What is time?

Everyone uses time. We cannot see it or hear it. We can waste it. We can measure it. But what is it? Why does it go forwards but never backwards?

People have asked these questions for thousands of **years**. Although nobody knows the answers, scientists are able to measure time more **accurately** than ever before.

Clocks and calendars

We use **clocks** and **watches** to show us the time – the **hours**, the **minutes** and the **seconds**. We use **calendars** to show us the date – the **day**, the **month** and the year.

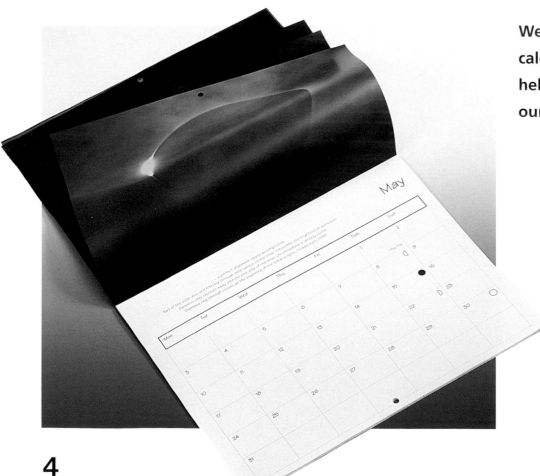

We use calendars to help us plan our lives.

4

Clocks and watches show the time in hours,
minutes and seconds.

More and more accurate clocks

Four hundred years ago, the best clocks would lose or gain
about 15 minutes a day. Your watch is probably about
1000 times more accurate, losing or gaining no more than
a second a day. Although this sounds impressive, it is
about 5,000,000,000 times less accurate than the world's
most accurate clocks. These will lose or gain no more than
a second in 15 million years.

Patterns in time

Days

The Earth is spinning on its **axis**. As it spins round, we get darkness, followed by daylight, followed by darkness again. The pattern of daylight and darkness repeats itself each time the Earth completes one full turn on its axis. This is because different parts of the Earth are facing the Sun at different times. Our **day** is based on this repeating pattern.

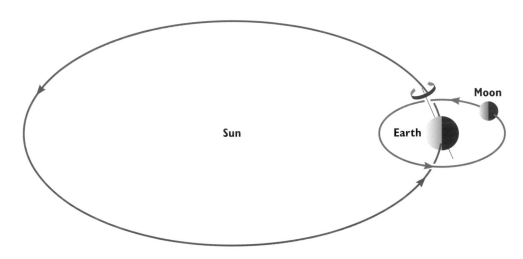

The length of our days, months and years are linked to the movements of the Earth and the Moon.

Months

The Moon **orbits** the Earth. Its appearance in the sky changes in a pattern from one day to the next. The pattern repeats itself each time the Moon passes in its orbit between the Earth and the Sun. Our **month** is based on this repeating pattern.

Years

The Earth orbits the Sun. As it goes on its journey around the Sun, we pass from one season to the next. The pattern of the seasons repeats itself each time the Earth starts a new orbit. Our **year** is based on this repeating pattern.

We get light and heat from the Sun. We also use the Sun to measure our days and years.

The appearance of the Moon changes as it orbits the Earth. The picture on the right was taken three days after the one on the left.

Hours and minutes

We divide our **day** into smaller parts called **hours**. In ancient times, the day was usually divided so that there were 12 hours of **daytime** and 12 hours of **night-time**. However daytime, or the time when the Sun is shining on our part of the Earth, is longer in the summer than in the winter. In the summer, daytime hours were longer than the night-time ones. In the winter, night-time hours were longer than daytime ones.

Today, we still divide our days into 24 hours. Now our hours are all the same length. Each hour is divided into 60 **minutes**. Each minute is divided into 60 **seconds**.

On most clocks and watches the hour hand goes round twice each day.

8

On a few clocks and watches, the hour hand goes round once every 24 hours.

The decimal day

About 200 years ago the French decided to change their day. Each of their days was divided into 10 hours. Each of these hours was more than twice the length of a normal hour. Each hour was divided into 100 minutes. Each minute was divided into 100 seconds. Many people in France and other countries didn't like this decimal day. In the end, the French stopped using it.

Calendars

Years

Our **year** is linked to the seasons. The pattern of the seasons repeats itself in just under $365\frac{1}{4}$ days. Because this is not a whole number of **days**, our **calendar** years have either 365 or 366 days. Years with 366 days are called **leap years**. They normally occur every four years. The extra day is added to the month of February.

Leap years

If the year number can be divided by four and it doesn't end in 00, the year is a leap year. If it ends in 00, it is only a leap year if it can be divided by 400. This means that 1900 wasn't a leap year, but 2000 was.

Months

Our **months** are linked to the movements of the Moon. The Moon passes between the Earth and the Sun every $29\frac{1}{2}$ days. When this happens, there is a new moon. In the Jewish and Muslim calendars, a new month starts. All Jewish and Muslim months have either 29 or 30 days.

A new crescent Moon appears at the start of each Jewish and Muslim month.

In the calendar we normally use, months are slightly longer. There are twelve of them in a year. Apart from February, they have either 30 or 31 days. Because of this, they rarely start on the same day as Jewish and Muslim months.

Thirty days hath September,
April, June and November,
All the rest have thirty-one,
Excepting February alone,
And that has twenty-eight days clear,
And twenty-nine in each leap year.

Different people divide up the year in slightly different ways. Today, for most purposes we all use the Christian calendar. It is based on the Roman calendar introduced by Julius Caesar a little over 2000 years ago. People who aren't Christians sometimes use their own religious calendar as well. Jewish and Muslim calendars are in use in different parts of the world.

Julius Caesar started our system of leap years.

11

The names of the months

Our **calendar** was started by the Romans. At first, there were just ten named **months**. There was a break between December and March. This break had no name. January and February were added later.

January is named after the Roman god Janus. Janus had two faces. One looked forward to the future, and one looked back to the past.

February is named after Februa, the Roman festival of purification.

March is named after Mars, the Roman god of war. In ancient Rome, it was the first month in the calendar.

Janus was the Roman god of doors, gates and new beginnings.

April comes from the Latin word *aperire*, which means to open. In Rome, the buds started to open in April at the start of spring.

May is named after the Roman goddess of growth, Maia.

June is named after the Roman goddess Juno. Juno was the queen of heaven.

July was originally called Quintilis, which means the fifth month. After January and February were added, it became the seventh month. Its name was changed to July in honour of Julius Caesar.

August was originally called Sextilis. Sextilis means the sixth month. It was renamed August to honour the Roman emperor Augustus.

September means the seventh month – it's now the ninth.

October means the eighth month – it's now the tenth.

November means the ninth month – it's now the eleventh.

December means the tenth month – it's now the twelfth.

Augustus was the first Roman emperor.

Day names

In many European languages, the names of the **days** of the **week** come from the old Roman names. The Romans named the days of the week after the Sun, the Moon, and the planets Mars, Mercury, Jupiter, Venus and Saturn. They believed that the Sun was a god, and named a day after him to keep him happy. Monday was named after the Moon. It was originally called the Moon's day. Saturday is named after the planet Saturn. We still use these Roman names for Sunday, Monday and Saturday.

**Saturn was the Roman god of farming.
Both Saturday and the planet Saturn
are named after him.**

In France, the days are named after the Sun, the Moon and the planets. Thursday *(jeudi)* is named after the planet Jupiter, the largest planet in the Solar System.

Our names for the other four days were later altered by the Anglo-Saxons. Tiw was their god of war. Tuesday is named after him. Wednesday is named after the god Woden. Woden was Tiw's father. He was the most powerful of the Anglo-Saxon gods. Thursday is named after the god Thor. Thor was the god of thunder and war. Friday is named after the goddess Frigg. Frigg was married to Woden, and was the goddess of marriage. The Anglo-Saxons thought Friday was a lucky day.

Day name	
Today	*In Saxon times*
Sunday	Sun's Day
Monday	Moon's Day
Tuesday	Tiw's Day
Wednesday	Woden's Day
Thursday	Thor's Day
Friday	Frigg's Day
Saturday	Saterne's Day

Timers

Timers are used to measure intervals of time. We use them in the kitchen to make sure our food is properly cooked. Some cooks use a sand timer when boiling an egg.

To start a sand timer, you have to turn it upside down. The sand in this timer takes one **minute** to run back down to the bottom.

A kitchen timer – unlike a clock it is unable to tell you the time of **day**. When the time is set it will measure short periods of time and an alarm will sound when the time has passed.

Pendulums

A swinging **pendulum** can be used as a timer. You can make one from a weight and a length of thread. The longer your pendulum is, the longer it will take to swing from side to side.

From timer to clock

You can use a timer, for example a pendulum, to tell the time. As well as counting the swings, you would have to make sure it didn't stop. You'd also need to know the time when you started counting.

Keeping track of the time is much easier with an automatic timer and counter – in other words, with a normal **clock** or a **watch**! Unlike you, they don't need to go to sleep!

A pendulum 99 centimetres long will swing from side to side in about a **second**. To time a minute, you would have to count 60 swings of the pendulum.

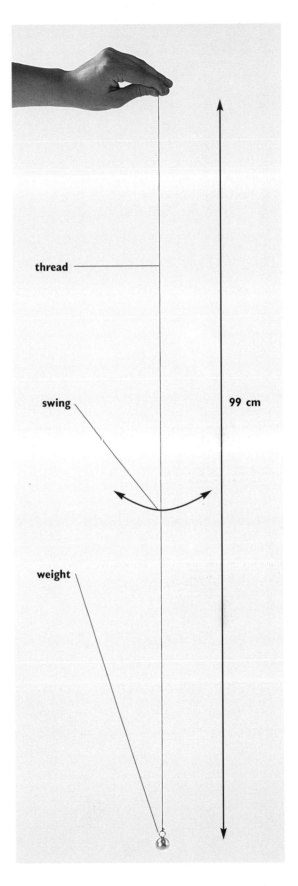

thread

swing

weight

99 cm

The first clocks

From the earliest times, people used the movement of the Sun across the sky to tell the time. A **sundial** casts a shadow which tells us the time by the position of the Sun.

The world's first mechanical **clocks** were made in Europe about 700 years ago. Most of them looked different to today's clocks. They told the time by ringing a bell – usually every **hour**. They were not very **accurate**. It was only later that hands were fitted. To start with, there was normally only an hour hand. It moved in the same direction that the Sun appears to move across the sky in the **northern hemisphere** – the direction we now call **clockwise**.

Until about 350 years ago, the timer used in most clocks was a metal bar called a foliot. It swung from side to side at a regular rate.

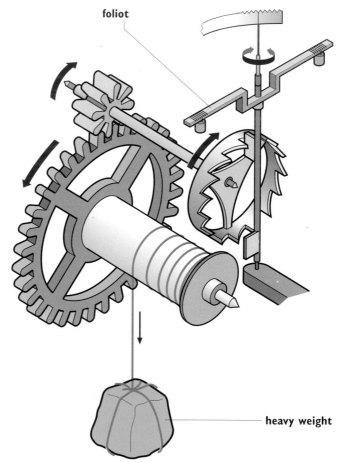

foliot

heavy weight

In the **southern hemisphere** the Sun always appears to move across the sky in the opposite direction – the direction we call **anticlockwise**. If clocks had been invented in Australia instead of Europe, clockwise and anticlockwise might be the opposite way round!

This type of clock is called a lantern clock. This one was made in the 1600s. It started life with a foliot timer. Its timekeeping improved when this was changed for a **pendulum** in the 1800s. The pendulum swings from side to side twice each **second**.

pendulum

This watch is about 350 years old. Like the lantern clock, it has an hour hand, but no **minute** hand.

19

Today's clocks and watches

Pendulum clocks

Pendulums have been used as **timers** in **clocks** since 1657. They are still used in a few clocks today. Some clocks have long pendulums which swing from side to side once each **second**. Others have shorter pendulums which swing at a faster rate. The clock ticks each time the pendulum swings from side to side.

Inside the clock there are lots of toothed wheels. Their job is to count the swings of the pendulum and make the hands move at the right rate.

pendulum

In this clock, the pendulum swings from side to side once every second.

Quartz clocks

The timer in almost all modern clocks and **watches** is a piece of **quartz** crystal. An electric current from the battery makes the crystal vibrate at a steady rate. In most quartz clocks and watches, it vibrates 32,768 times each second. An electronic circuit counts the vibrations. Every time 32,768 vibrations are counted, the second hand moves one step round the **dial**.

A quartz watch.

Battery

The quartz timer is hidden from view inside this container

Most of today's alarm clocks contain a quartz timer.

Astronomers and timekeeping

We rely on scientists and **astronomers** to provide us with the exact time when we need it. They work out the time by measuring how far the Earth has turned on its **axis**. Until the 1970s, they did this using specially-designed **telescopes** like the one shown below. The telescopes could only point in a north–south direction. They could be moved up and down but not from side to side.

Until recently, most **observatories** had a telescope like this for finding the exact time. This one was used at the Royal Observatory, Greenwich, London between 1816 and 1850.

Timekeeper Earth

As the Earth turns on its axis, the stars appear to move across the sky in a similar way to the Sun. Every time the Earth completes one full turn on its axis, the same stars reappear in front of the telescope.

Astronomers used the Earth, the stars and the telescope like a **clock**. The Earth was the **timer** – spinning on its axis once each **day**. The telescope was the clock hand and the stars were the numbers around the **dial**.

Nowadays, astronomers measure how far the Earth has turned by measuring the positions of **satellites**. The satellites are tracked using telescopes that can be turned to point anywhere in the sky.

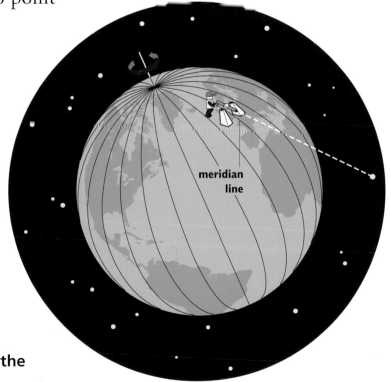

meridian
line

Using the Earth, the stars and a telescope to find the correct time.

What's the time?

In the past, it was much more difficult than it is today to set a **clock** or **watch** to exactly the right time. Clocks were normally checked with a **sundial**. At best, sundials can be used to set a clock to about the nearest **minute**. People who needed to know the time more **accurately** had to use a special **telescope** or visit an **observatory**.

Between the 1830s and the 1930s, some clockmakers in London checked their clocks each week, using an accurate watch belonging to the Belville family. Ruth Belville is shown here checking her watch at the Royal Observatory Greenwich – something she did each Monday morning.

Before watches became widely available, wealthy people would often use a portable sundial like this.

Time signals

Today, we can set our watches to the nearest fraction of a **second** using a television or radio. Many radio stations transmit a special time signal to tell people the precise time. The world's first radio time signals were transmitted by the American navy in 1904.

The first British time signals were transmitted by the BBC in 1924. They came from the Royal Observatory in Greenwich. They marked the **hours** of **Greenwich Mean Time**. Today, they normally consist of six pips, spaced one second apart. The last pip is longer than the rest and is the time mark.

This radio-controlled clock contains a built-in radio receiver and automatically adjusts itself to the correct time.

25

Atomic clocks

More accurate than the Earth

Atomic clocks are the most **accurate clocks** ever built. The first one was built about 50 years ago. They run at a steadier rate than the Earth. Their incredible accuracy led scientists to change the way in which they measure and describe the length of a **second**.

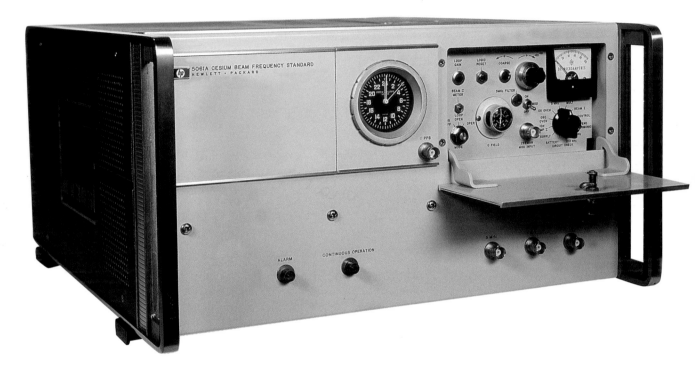

This caesium-atomic clock will lose or gain no more than one second in 300,000 years.

The length of a second

A hundred **years** ago, a second was said to be 1/86,400 of an average **day**. Since 1967, scientists have described it as the time taken for 9,192,631,770 vibrations of the **timer** inside a caesium-atomic clock to occur.

Leap seconds

Little by little, our Earth is slowing down. Scientists use **satellites** and atomic clocks to measure how fast this is happening. In 1972, they decided to make some days one second longer than normal. They did this to prevent the Earth and the time shown by our clocks from getting out of step. The extra seconds are called **leap seconds**. There has been one added in most years since 1972. Radio-controlled clocks adjust themselves automatically when leap seconds are added.

Today's time signals are produced using atomic clocks. They give us accurate time. We do not have to own an atomic clock of our own.

Mobile phone networks and satellite navigation systems need accurate timing systems. If there were no atomic clocks, neither system would work.

Factfile

If our Earth spun faster on its **axis**, our **days** would be shorter, and there would be more of them in a **year**!

Jupiter is the fastest-spinning planet and has the shortest days.

The **pendulum** in a long-case (grandfather) **clock** swings from side to side 86,400 times a day and over 31 million times a year!

The further a planet is from the Sun, the longer it takes to complete one **orbit**, and the longer its year is. The Earth is further from the Sun than Mercury, so its years are longer.

Nobody knew for certain that the Earth was spinning on its axis at a steady rate until 1676. In that year, John Flamsteed checked that it did. He used clocks and a **telescope** at the Royal **Observatory**, Greenwich, London.

If the Earth was as far away from the Sun as Pluto, it would complete less than half an orbit in your entire lifetime. You would die before your first birthday!

John Flamsteed at the Royal Observatory, Greenwich.

This was the first **watch** able to keep **accurate** time at sea. It allowed a sailor out of sight of land to calculate his position accurately. This had never been possible before. The watch was built by John Harrison and was first tested at sea in 1761. It eventually won him a prize of £20,000 – equivalent to you winning the lottery today.

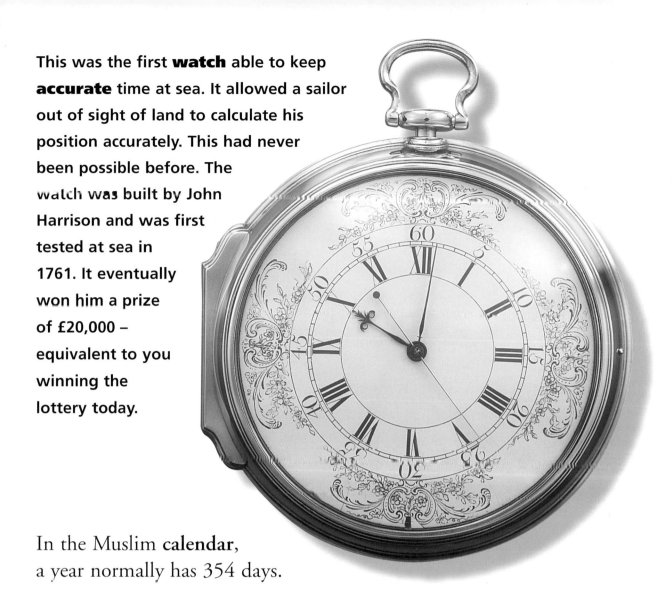

In the Muslim **calendar**, a year normally has 354 days.

In the Jewish calendar, some years have 12 **months**. Others have 13.

When the system of **leap years** first started, a mistake was made and they were inserted every three years instead of every four.

Some years are longer than others. The year 1992 was longer than 1996, which was longer than 1997, which was longer than 1999! Can you think why?

A few weeks after your 57th birthday, you will have been alive for half a million hours!

Glossary

accurate an accurate clock or watch is one where the difference between the time shown and the actual time is always very small

anticlockwise the opposite direction to the way in which the hands on a clock move

astronomer someone who observes or studies the stars and planets

atomic clock the most accurate type of clock that has ever been built

axis an imaginary line passing through the North and South Poles and the centre of a planet, around which the planet spins

calendar the division of the year into days, weeks and months

clock a device for measuring time

clockwise the direction in which the hands of a clock move

day a length of time based on the time it takes for the Earth to spin round once on its axis

daytime the time between sunrise and sunset

dial the part of a clock or watch which shows the time

foliot a swinging bar used as a timer in the clocks made by the first clockmakers

Greenwich Mean Time originally this was the accurate time, as calculated in and used by the Royal Observatory Greenwich. The British chose it as the time for legal use in 1880, and time in all the countries of the world became based on it.

hour a length of time – there are 24 hours in a day

leap second an extra second that is added from time to time to keep our clocks in step with the gradually slowing Earth

leap year a year with 366 days

minute a length of time – there are 60 minutes in an hour

midday the time when the Sun reaches its highest point of the day

month a length of time based on the time it takes for the Moon to orbit the Earth once

night-time the time between sunset and sunrise

northern hemisphere the half of the Earth north of the Equator

observatory a building where astronomers make observations with telescopes and other instruments

orbit the path of a planet around the Sun or a moon around a planet

pendulum   a swinging wooden or metal rod (or length of thread) with a weight attached to its lower end. Pendulums are used as timers in some clocks.

phase of the Moon   the shape of the lit portion of the Moon as seen from the Earth

quartz   a crystalline mineral. A quartz timer is used in most modern clocks and watches

second   a length of time – there are 60 seconds in a minute

southern hemisphere   the half of the Earth south of the Equator

sundial   a device that uses shadows to find the time from the Sun's position in the sky

telescope   an instrument that makes distant objects appear nearer and larger

timer   a device used for measuring a specific interval of time

vibrate   to move rapidly to and fro

watch   a small timekeeper which has been designed to be carried about or worn

week   a length of time – there are seven days in a week

year   a length of time based on the time taken for the Earth to orbit the Sun once and for the cycle of seasons to repeat itself. A normal calendar year has 365 days. A leap year has 366 days.

Index